Land Mammals

ANIMAL FACTS

by Heather C. Hudak

WEIGL PUBLISHERS INC.

Published by Weigl Publishers Inc.
350 5th Avenue, Suite 3304, PMB 6G
New York, NY 10118-0069 USA
Web site: www.weigl.com

Copyright 2005 WEIGL PUBLISHERS INC.
All rights reserved. No part of this publication may be reproduced, stored in a retrieval system, or transmitted in any form or by any means, electronic, mechanical, photocopying, recording, or otherwise, without the prior written permission of the publisher.

Library of Congress Cataloging-in-Publication Data

Hudak, Heather C., 1975-
   Land mammals / Heather C. Hudak.
      p. cm. -- (Animal facts)
   Includes bibliographical references (p.   ).
   ISBN 1-59036-200-4 (lib. bdg. : alk. paper) 1-59036-245-4 (softcover)
1. Mammals--Juvenile literature. I. Title. II. Series.
   QL706.2.H84 2004
   599--dc22
                              2004001954

Printed in the United States of America
1 2 3 4 5 6 7 8 9 0   08 07 06 05 04

Project Coordinator Heather C. Hudak   **Substantive Editor** Janice L. Redlin
Copy Editor Tina Schwartzenberger   **Design** Janine Vangool
Layout Bryan Pezzi   **Photo Researcher** Ellen Bryan

Photograph and Text Credits
Every reasonable effort has been made to trace ownership and to obtain permission to reprint copyright material. The publishers would be pleased to have any errors or omissions brought to their attention so that they may be corrected in subsequent printings.

Cover: Photos.com; **Calgary Zoo:** page 18; **Corel Corporation:** pages 4, 7B, 15, 17L, 20, 23; **DigitalVision:** page 19B; **Eileen Herrling:** page 9T; **Photos.com:** pages 1, 7T, 11T, 11B, 17R, 21, 22; **Dan Nedrelo:** pages 9B, 14B; **J.D. Taylor:** pages 3, 5, 6T, 6B, 16; **Kevin Schafer Photography:** page 10; **A.B. Sheldon:** page 12; **Tom Stack & Associates/Dave Watts:** pages 8, 13, 14T, 19T.

All of the Internet URLs given in the book were valid at the time of publication. However, due to the dynamic nature of the Internet, some addresses may have changed, or sites may have ceased to exist since publication. While the author and publisher regret any inconvenience this may cause readers, no responsibility for any such changes can be accepted by either the author or the publisher.

Contents

What Is a Land Mammal? 4

Land Mammal Lot 6

Land Mammal Looks 8

Land Mammal Lineage 10

Life Cycle 12

Land Mammal Lairs 14

Land Mammal Morsels 16

Threatened Land Mammals 18

Activities 20

Quiz 22

Further Reading/Web Sites 23

Glossary/Index 24

What Is a Land Mammal?

Impalas are mammals that live in the southern part of Africa.

The Javan rhinoceros lives only in Indonesia, Vietnam, and on the island of Java.

Mammals are warm-blooded animals. Mammals have lived on Earth for millions of years. There are about 4,600 mammal **species** alive today. While most mammals live on land, some live in the water. Land mammals share some common features.

Nearly all mammals are covered with fur or hair. They also have special teeth called molars. These teeth help mammals chew or cut their food. Most mammals give birth to live babies. All young mammals need their mothers. Mothers produce milk that they use to nurse, or feed, their babies. Mammals are vertebrates. This means they have backbones.

There are many types of land mammals. Humans are mammals. Bats, dogs, giraffes, hamsters, and kangaroos are mammals, too.

Fast Facts

The Javan rhinoceros is the world's rarest land mammal. There are only 50 to 60 Javan rhinoceroses on Earth.

African elephants are the largest land mammals. They weigh about 6.06 tons (5.5 metric tonnes). They stand about 10.5 feet (3.2 meters) tall at the shoulder.

The smallest non-flying mammal is the pygmy white-toothed shrew. It is 1.4 inches (3.5 centimeters) long.

Land Mammal Lot

There are three groups of land mammals. These groups are *monotremes*, *marsupials*, and *placentals*.

Monotremes lay eggs. Young monotremes hatch from the eggs. The young feed on their mother's milk. Monotremes are the smallest mammal group. There are three monotreme species. They are the duckbill **platypus** and two types of echidnas, or spiny anteaters. Monotremes, such as this echidna, live in Australia, New Guinea, and Tasmania.

Marsupials carry their young in a pouch. The pouch is part of the mother's body. Young marsupials are not fully formed. The baby lives in the pouch until it develops. This can take weeks or months. There are about 250 marsupial species. Most marsupials live in Australia. The quokka kangaroo, pictured here, is a marsupial.

Blesboks are a type of antelope that live in the high grasslands of South Africa. They are placental mammals.

Placentals develop inside their mother's bodies. There, they feed off the **placenta**. Placental babies are fully formed at birth. Placentals are the largest mammal group. There are about 4,300 placental species. There are 19 placental **orders**. The largest order is the rodents, such as rats and mice. There are 1,500 rodent species. Another order is called carnivores. These are meat-eating animals. There are 240 carnivore species. Humans belong to the primate order. Monkeys and apes are primates, too. There are 230 primate species. The patas monkey, pictured here, is a placental.

Land Mammal Looks

Mammals have three basic body features. Mammals have skin or fur. They have a skeleton that protects their **vital organs**. They also have internal organ systems, such as the heart and blood cells, the brain, lungs, and stomach. Some mammals have unique features that help them live in different parts of the world.

Platypuses are also called duckbills. They use their bill to stir up mud at the bottom of rivers when searching for the insects, worms, and shellfish they eat.

Monotremes often look like **reptiles**. Platypuses are monotremes. Waterproof fur covers their bodies. They also have webbed feet and bills. Males have poisonous spikes on their ankles. These spikes protect them against enemies. Spiny anteaters have spines to protect them from **predators**. They have sticky tongues, too. This helps them pick up ants and worms for food.

Marsupials come in many shapes and sizes. Marsupials have short front legs and long hind, or back, legs. They move by hopping. Some marsupials may look like rodents, dogs, or cats. Marsupials have smaller brains than other mammals.

There are many types of placentals. There are some placentals that fly. Bats use wings to fly. Other placentals have hoofed feet and antlers. These include camels, cows, deer, and pigs. A few types of placentals have **opposable thumbs**. For example, humans use their thumbs to hold objects. Placentals are the most common mammals. They come in all shapes and sizes.

Eastern gray kangaroos can jump up to 29.5 feet (9 meters) in a single leap.

Orangutans use their hook-shaped hands for grasping vines and branches. They use their opposable thumbs to collect food and to build nests where they can sleep.

Fast Facts

The kangaroo is the largest marsupial. It can weigh more than 176.4 pounds (80 kg). It can stand 6 feet (1.83 m) tall.

The smallest mammal is the kitti's hog-nosed bat. It weighs only 0.05 ounces (1.4 grams).

Land Mammal Lineage

Scientists use **fossils** to learn about animal history. They have found some mammal fossils. Scientists use these fossils to study the first mammals. They still need to learn more about these animals.

Mammals developed from reptiles. These reptiles were called *synapsids*. Synapsids lived 325 million years ago. Over time, *therapsids* developed. Therapsids lived about 200 million years ago. They were mammal-like reptiles. *Cynodonts* were a group of therapsids. Cynodonts were the first mammals. They had teeth, skulls, and limbs like mammals.

Notoungulata were a group of mammals that lived in South America more than 60 million years ago. They were ungulates, or hoofed mammals, much like horses.

One of the first mammals was *Morganucodon*. This animal lived about 200 million years ago. Morganucodon looked like a small weasel. It was about 1 inch (2.5 centimeters) tall and 4 inches (10.16 cm) long. It was active at night. It ate insects and small animals.

Bat fossils from more than 50 million years ago look very much like modern bats. Bats are the only flying mammals.

Fast Facts

Mammals lived on Earth for millions of years before dinosaurs lived.

Reptile teeth are one size. Mammal teeth are many shapes and sizes.

Human arms, seal flippers, and bat wings all have the same number of bones.

Baboons' teeth allow them to eat worms, eggs, insects, reptiles, crabs, and mollusks.

Life Cycle

Red kangaroos can live as long as 18 years. Male red kangaroos have reddish coats. Female red kangaroos have blue-gray fur. These females are sometimes called blue fliers.

Most mammals do not hatch from eggs. They are born live. Female mammals produce eggs. The male **fertilizes** the egg inside the female's body. Nearly all placentals grow their young inside their bodies. Female mammals produce milk to feed their young. Over time, they **wean** their young. The young mammals learn to survive on their own. Mature mammals mate to produce young.

Monotremes hatch from eggs. The young are not well developed. They cling to the fur on their mother's belly. Here, they feed on her milk. The milk comes from pores, or tiny openings, in the mother's skin.

Marsupials start to develop inside their mothers. When they are born, they climb up their mother's fur to a pouch. They settle inside the pouch. They feed on milk inside the pouch. They leave the pouch once they have finished developing.

Echidnas lay one or two eggs at a time. They place the egg in a pouch on their stomach area. After the egg hatches, the young echidna lives in the mother's pouch until it is able to walk.

13

Land Mammal Lairs

Mammals live in all parts of the world. They live in many **habitats**. Some live in the freezing Arctic. Others live in hot, dry deserts. Many live in grasslands, or large grassy areas. Mammals live in places where there is plenty of food.

Platypuses live in streams and rivers. Females raise their young in burrows.

Wombats hide face down in dens or hollow logs. The thick skin on their rump protects them from a predator's teeth and claws.

Monotremes live only in Australia, New Guinea, and Tasmania. Echidnas are found in every type of habitat. They are found in deserts, forests, and hilly areas called highlands. Echidnas live in thick bushes, hollow logs, and under rocks.

Most marsupials live in Australia. Some live on nearby islands such as Tasmania and New Guinea. The wombat is a marsupial. It lives in **savanna forests** and grasslands. The wombat digs burrows, or holes and tunnels. It builds a grassy nest at the end of the burrow.

Placental mammals live in every part of the world. Placentals may live in trees. Squirrels make nests from leaves and twigs. Raccoons live in hollow trees and branches. Other placentals live underground. Moles dig burrows in the soil. Some placentals live near wetlands. Beavers live in or near the water. They settle near rivers and streams. Beavers use their teeth to build dams from tree branches. Dams protect their homes from washing away.

Raccoons live across North and South America. Northern raccoons make their homes in forests near lakes and streams. They often live near towns and cities.

Fast Facts

The Virginia opossum is the only marsupial in North America. Marsupials do not live in Europe, Asia, or Africa.

Gray foxes can climb trees. They often hide in trees.

Land Mammal Morsels

Mammals must eat to stay warm. Some mammals eat only plants. Others eat meat, too.

There are some small mammals that eat insects. Anteaters use their sense of sight or smell to find food. They use their sticky tongues to gather thousands of ants or termites in just a few minutes.

Anteaters have long tubular mouths that allow them to stick their tongues deep into termite nests and anthills.

Koalas are herbivores. These are plant-eating animals. Koalas are fussy eaters. They eat only a few types of **gum leaves**. They must live in the places where these trees grow. Koalas eat 7 ounces to 18 oz (198.4 to 510.3 grams) of leaves each day.

Koalas sniff each gum leaf before choosing one to eat.

Adult gray wolves and red wolves have 42 teeth. Adult humans only have 32 teeth.

Wolves are carnivores. They have pointed front teeth called canines. Canines help wolves hold their food. Wolves have special back teeth, too. These teeth help wolves slice through their food. Wolves eat deer. They eat mice, rabbits, and birds, too. Wolves eat a large amount of fruit in the summer.

Fast Facts

Some animals are omnivores. This means they eat both plants and meat. Chimpanzees eat mostly fruit. They may eat deer, bush pigs, and baboons, too.

Tigers are the largest land mammals with an all-meat diet.

Hyenas eat every part of an animal. They even eat the bones.

Giraffes are ungulates. Ungulates spend 75 percent of their lives eating.

Threatened Land Mammals

Animals that are in danger of becoming **extinct** are called endangered. This means there are so few of the species that they need protection in order to survive. People are not allowed to hunt endangered species in the United States.

There are only about 1,000 giant pandas living in nature. About 140 live in zoos around the world.

There are many endangered mammals. In some cases, their habitat has become too **polluted** and unhealthy. Other habitats have disappeared. Some mammals have been overhunted.

The giant panda is endangered. Humans hunted the giant panda for thousands of years.

The giant panda once lived in Vietnam, Myanmar, and China. Today, it lives only in six mountain ranges in China. Loss of habitat is the giant panda's main threat. Humans are using the panda's land for farming. Some pandas become trapped in deer hunters' snares. Others cannot find enough **bamboo** to eat.

The bilby once lived in many parts of Australia. Hunters trapped and poisoned the bilby for its skin. Now the bilby is endangered. Bilbies are losing their habitats. They must compete with other animals for food and shelter. Humans are trying to protect the bilbies' habitat. They are breeding bilbies and moving them to new areas, too.

Animals that eat human garbage may forget how to search for food in nature.

Bilbies once lived throughout Australia's dry regions. Today, bilbies live only in Australia's northern deserts.

Fast Facts

About 500 animals are endangered in the United States.

About 11,000 mammal species are threatened with extinction.

Activities

Mammal Name Game

There are many land mammal species. Some are large. Others are small. Each has a different name. Play the following game to learn land mammal names.

Materials
- Timer

1. Sit in a circle with at least two other people.
2. Set the time for 30 to 45 seconds.
3. Pass the timer around the circle. The person holding the timer must say the name of a mammal. Be quick. If you name another kind of animal, try again. Keep trying until you name a mammal. Then, pass the timer to the next person.

Gray fox pups begin to hunt with their parents when they are 3 months old. When these pups are 4 months old, they begin to look for food on their own.

4. Keep a list of the other animals named. Explain why these are not mammals. What kind of animals are they?
5. The person holding the timer when it stops is out of the game. This person should step out of the circle.
6. Repeat until only one person is left playing the game. This person is the Mammal Expert.

Mammal Mobile

Do you know the difference between land mammals and other animal groups? For example, did you know that a zebra is a land mammal and a dolphin is a marine mammal? Try the following activity to see how much you know about land mammals and other animals.

Materials

- animal pictures
- twig
- cardboard
- string
- crayons
- construction paper
- glue
- scissors
- hole punch

1. Cut out several animal pictures.

2. Glue each picture to a separate piece of cardboard. Punch a hole at the top.

3. Thread each hole with a piece of string. Tie the string to the twig. Place mammals on one side of the twig and non-mammals on the other side.

4. Write facts about the animals on pieces of construction paper. Hang the facts on the twig, too.

Both male and female caribou have antlers. Females have smaller antlers than males.

Quiz

What have you learned about land mammals? See if you can answer the following questions correctly.

1. How many types of mammals are there?

2. Where do mammals live?

3. What do mammals eat?

4. From what animal did mammals develop?

5. What features do all mammals share?

Cheetahs are one of the fastest land mammals. They can travel at speeds up to 58 mph (93.3 kmph) for as far as 1,000 feet (305 m).

Answers: 1. There are three types of land mammals. They are placentals, marsupials, and monotremes. 2. Mammals live in all parts of the world. Some live in the freezing Arctic. Others live in the dry desert. 3. Mammals eat insects, plants, or meat. 4. Land mammals developed from reptiles called synapsids. 5. All land mammals have skin or fur, a skeleton, and an internal organ system.

Further Reading

Bailey, Jacqui, Joe Elliot (editor), and Jayne Miller (editor). *Amazing Animal Facts*. New York, NY: DK Publishing, 2003.

Parker, Steve, Dave King (photographer), and Jane Burton (photographer). *Eyewitness: Mammal*. New York, NY: DK Publishing, 2000.

Web Sites

To learn more about mammals, visit
www.enchantedlearning.com/subjects/mammals/Mammals.shtml

For more information about mammals, surf to
www.abdn.ac.uk/mammal/newsite/index.shtml

Elephants can travel up to 6,200 miles (9,978 km) each year in search of food.

Glossary

bamboo grasses that have hard stems and grow as tall as trees

extinct no longer living any place on Earth

fertilizes makes another animal able to produce young

fossils rocklike remains of ancient plants and animals

gum leaves the leaves of certain plants

habitats places where animals live in nature

opposable thumbs thumbs that can face and touch the end of one or more fingers on the same hand

orders the way things are organized or arranged

placenta an organ that feeds an unborn baby

platypus mammal with a wide bill, long, flat tail, and webbed feet

polluted made unfit or harmful

predators animals that eat the flesh of other animals

reptiles cold-blooded animals

savanna forests tropical and subtropical grasslands where trees sometimes grow

species type or sort

vital organs essential parts of the body

wean to slowly stop feeding a baby its mother's milk

Index

carnivores 7, 17

echidna 6, 13, 14
eggs 6, 11, 13
elephant 5, 23
endangered 18, 19

food 5, 8, 9, 14, 16, 17, 19, 20, 23

habitats 14, 18, 19
herbivores 17

koala 17

life cycle 12, 13

marsupials 6, 9, 13, 14, 15, 22
monotremes 6, 8, 13, 14, 22

omnivores 17

placentals 6, 7, 9, 13, 15, 22
platypus 6, 8, 14